A GIFT FOR

....

FROM

....

Dedication:

With love for my daughters and nieces, the next generation of vibrant women in our family:

Johanna, Isabel, Alyssa, Olivia, Kara, Krista, Kelly, Kyle, Ellse, and Kajsa

May each of you continue to grow in faith, wisdom, strength, and in love with our Heavenly Father.

New Baby, New Love

Copyright © Bonnie Sparrman

Published by KPT Publishing
Minneapolis, Minnesota 55406
www.KPTPublishing.com

Scripture quotations marked (NIV) are taken from THE HOLY BIBLE, NEW INTERNATIONAL VERSION®, NIV® Copyright © 1973, 1978, 1984, 2011 by Biblica, Inc.® Used by permission. All rights reserved worldwide.

ISBN 978-1-944833-38-1

Cover/interior design by
Koechel Peterson and Associates, Minneapolis, Minnesota.

First printing April 2018
10 9 8 7 6 5 4 3 2 1

Printed in the United States of America

New Baby,
New Love

Tender expressions for a new mom

BONNIE SPARRMAN

KPT PUBLISHING

Introduction

If pregnancy teaches anything, it is patience. The same goes for the bumpy journey of adoption, which is often punctuated by frustrating starts and stops. Anticipation and suspense holds all new moms tightly as we prepare our nest and wait for the baby. Through it all, the patience we learn comes in handy when we hold that beautiful baby in our arms.

Bringing a baby home is to welcome a sweet little person who steals our heart, yet unabashedly rearranges the calendar, bank account, living space, and any relationship. No matter the excitement, we need patience and perseverance as we transition to parenthood for the first time or even when adding one more baby to our brood.

If you feel terrified as you embark on the journey of motherhood, know that you are not alone. Even working in a newborn nursery did not prepare me for bringing home our first baby. To care for an infant around the clock seemed frightening, and taking full responsibility for our newborn's life without the support of my colleagues at the hospital was surprisingly foreign. Here I was, as green as any other young mom, and I was exhausted—overwhelmed—by the multitude of new challenges that filled my days and nights.

Hormones swirled, laundry mounted, and I struggled with feelings of failure. Looking back, the experience seemed as difficult as it was beautiful. Friends surrounded and supported me, and my own mom came to help me find my way, but perhaps my greatest help was the opportunity to nurture my faith in God during the baby's frequent feedings. This kept me going.

When I sat down to feed the baby, I had a few quiet moments to pray and read snippets from the Bible. These little breaks provided just enough spiritual sustenance to survive the long days and nights, even when sleep was precious and elusive. While the baby received nourishment, so did I. This wonderful, holy double-tasking—the baby feeding physically, and myself spiritually, inspired the writing of this book. It is a gathering of short meditations intended to buoy the hearts of newborn moms who may be tired and in need of encouragement.

Don't be surprised if your reading is fragmented; if you read for just a few minutes, you're doing amazingly well. You will probably doze off a few times. Eventually, as you feed your little one, you will find emotional and spiritual nourishment for yourself through the words of a regular mom (me), who happens to draw joy and strength from her relationship with God.

This season of your life is fleeting. As you mother your baby, remember to stay well-fed both in body and spirit, and stick close to friends who help you laugh. Trust your instincts, be good to yourself, and know that you are a much-loved child of God. Let the words from the ancient book of Joshua encourage you: "Be strong and courageous. Do not be afraid; do not be discouraged, for the Lord your God will be with you wherever you go" (Joshua 1:9, NIV).

Bonnie Sparrman

The Apple of His Eye

Keep me as the apple of your eye;
hide me in the shadow of your wings.

PSALM 17:8, NIV

I remember a time when having babies was something my friends did, and I didn't understand what all the fuss was about. They would yammer about ridiculous things like diaper rash, homemade baby food, teething, and breast pumps. I felt completely bored and checked out of the conversation. Women I knew as perfectly intelligent professionals suddenly became mothers, completely losing their minds over infants who seemingly did nothing but eat, sleep, and poop. The most confusing part was the sincere, rapturous love each had for her own baby—the one most exceptional baby in the entire world.

My cynicism whispered they can't all be right, and inwardly I vowed to never become such a sappy mother. Then it happened. I became a mom, and that absurd, baby-obsessed zealot I swore to never become. My mind never ceased to revolve around my new baby. The funny part: I loved it, as absurd as it may seem. I joined their ranks knowing our baby Johanna was the prettiest little girl in the hospital nursery—ever! I marveled at the way she drew up her mouth into a perfect rosebud, and I adored her swirl of dark hair and deep blue eyes. I was smitten, and my friends heard all about this lovely baby girl who stole my heart. Still, I contemplated the question that continued to baffle me. How can each baby be the most beautiful ever?

Then I became pregnant with our second child, and I worried that I couldn't fall head-over-heels in love with this one as I had with our first. But when the doctor handed me baby Bjorn with his thick mop-top and soft cooing—indicating his mellow disposition—my heart soared with a new love I didn't know I had. A year and some months later, when our third baby burst on the scene, the great miracle happened all over again! My heart exploded, overflowing with joy over Karl-Jon—so beautiful and sweet he made me cry.

This perplexing journey into motherhood taught me that all mothers see their baby as the most adorable creature ever. It seems impossible that each little one is so uniquely special, but then again, why not? This deep attachment that I didn't understand before becoming a mom caught me by surprise. It's God's perfect provision, assuring that each baby receives the love and care needed to thrive.

As a new mother, consider the extraordinary affection that prompts every new mom to lavishly love her child. May we tread closer to understanding the beautiful, wild idea that God sees each of us as His perfect child. He is terribly fond of each one of us because we are His. Considering how parents love each baby with abandon, may we see with greater clarity that in God's eyes, every single individual is special, worthy of love, and the apple of His eye.

Leaving Perfect to God

Every good and perfect gift is from above,
coming down from the Father of the heavenly lights,
who does not change like shifting shadows.

JAMES 1:17, NIV

S taring into the perfectly beautiful face of our baby, we see the most breathtaking handiwork of God. Two bright eyes, a darling button nose, softly rounded cheeks, a rosebud mouth, and chubby chin—dimpled or not. Ten little fingers and ten tiny toes wait to expand and explore, and behold the belly button—the mark reminding us of our connection and constant nourishing from the beginning of conception. That alone should cause any mom's heart to soar in awe of the perfect loveliness of God's creation of this child. His child . . . our child. In such a gift we receive, it's hard to comprehend these feelings as parenthood begins and this child bears our name.

A baby is truly a good and perfect gift, entrusted to us by our Heavenly Father, and whether she arrived through adoption or your own delivery, our heart bursts with pride over this perfect little one in our hand, but we are also humbled at God's perfect workmanship. This epiphany leaves us feeling an enormous responsibility to care for something so valuable—so unblemished—we dare not make mistakes with this gift. We want to do this right.

But let's be real. God is God, and we are not. We are human; therefore, we define imperfection. Before we wear ourselves out with tall orders of flawless motherhood, let's understand from the get-go that we will not always do everything right. You will mess up. Days will come when weariness makes us cross, short-tempered, forgetful, or a bit nutty as hormones push us to fly off the handle over trivial frustrations. Balancing the tasks of motherhood with the ones already on your plate, some areas will slip, causing you to prioritize and reprioritize as you attempt to juggle your load.

It is humbling to allow an impeccably neat home become a mess, a tidy car collect crumbs and vomit stains, and even a perfectly flat stomach get a little "poochy." If no one has told you, if you birthed your baby, your body will never be exactly the same again. Even when you return to your pre-birth weight, your silhouette will be slightly altered. It's okay! Wouldn't we rather have a beautiful baby than a perfect body? Absolutely.

We all live somewhere on the scale of perfectionism. Some of us are perfectly satisfied with just the simplest of accomplishments and pleasures, while others hold themselves to stratospheric standards, but the fact is we all must deal with flaws in ourselves. None of us gets it right all the time. Every mom I've ever known tries desperately to rise to the mothering challenge—to be the best they can be for their child. It is a God-given instinct to care, protect, and provide, which is what "to mother" means. But God isn't looking for us to be the perfect ones; He is perfect enough for us all and would rather see us faithful in the midst of our flaws, rather than frustrated in pursuit of perfection.

Coincidence or Answered Prayer?

I sought the LORD and he heard me
and delivered me from all my fears.

PSALM 34:4, NIV

When I was eight months pregnant and with a seventeen-month-old strapped into the back seat of our Volkswagen, my husband and I drove from our home on the cool shores of Lake Michigan to steamy, blistering Washington D.C. The journey was far from an August vacation; we were moving for my husband's job. I was less than excited to have four weeks in which to find a new physician and new hospital in a strange city where I had no friends or family. "What a ridiculous situation," I thought bitterly as I began my last month of pregnancy.

Like most moves, the journey had its moments. When our movers put every box marked "nursery" in the basement and basement boxes upstairs in the nursery, I switched them in a fit of angry nesting. When my husband came home from work and discovered what I did, he thought I had taken an unnecessary risk. But a nesting mother is a force to be reckoned with, and I can assure you that one who is not happy about moving is fierce. That evening a neighbor saw me lower my aching frame into a tiny blow-up pool in our front yard and offered us passes to a local swim club. What a gift!

When my contractions started, a brand-new friend came to babysit our toddler so we could go to the hospital. Talk about help. She cared for our daughter and, along with a couple of other dear women whom we met at church, became a surrogate grandparent who loved our kids when our own parents lived far away. Once again, God provided, and He continued to over and over in all kinds of unpredictable ways, proving He is in control even when we think our situation is ridiculous.

Not only had we found awesome friends who loved our children, but you can imagine my shock when the nurse who cared for me after the delivery knew my mother, who lived hundreds of miles away in Chicago. What are the chances that this nurse and my mom had been obstetric nurses together for many years? When my mom arrived just hours after our baby was born, there was more than one reunion in my hospital room. My mom met her new grandson and reunited with a former nursing colleague. Hugs and tears were shared all around while I held our new son and shook my head at God's sense of humor. He calmed my fears.

Some may call this a coincidence—a well-timed small world story—but I choose to chalk it up to the answered prayers of many who knew I was unnerved at having to move far from my trusted physician and the hospital where I worked, at thirty-six weeks. Everything that gave me peace of mind was hundreds of miles away, yet God held me in His hands and worked through every detail of our transition. Were the blessings of this smooth delivery coincidental or were prayers answered? Yes, and yes! "Coincidences" like this one seem to happen more often when we commit the details of our lives to God in prayer.

What?

So do not fear, for I am with you;
do not be dismayed for I am your God.
I will strengthen you and help you;
I will uphold you with my righteous right hand.

ISAIAH 41:10, NIV

As a new mom, do you ever wonder what to do next? What needs my attention most? Is it the house, the baby, the nursery? Could it possibly be me? With a baby, the days are full and the list of chores is mind-boggling. We find very little time to do the things we used to do. Don't be shocked if you desperately need a haircut, and going to the gym feels like a thing of the distant past. We moms move from task to task all day long, meaning many of the jobs we do are cyclical, being done and undone in rapid succession, almost hypnotically. We wash lots of little clothes that are soiled again and again without thinking, and we make sure our infant swallows an adequate amount of milk only to dab up half of each feeding from under baby chins and off our own clothes

and floors. Some days, the monotony of it all threatens to thwart our sanity.

Our job description has soared off the charts as we bath, dress, feed, burp, swaddle, rock, walk, cuddle, and comfort. Plus, we make appointments, keep appointments, and learn about new things that never crossed our minds before. We attempt to make sense of immunizations, to understand why a three-month-old baby needs clothes marked "six months," and how to rid the baby's scalp of cradle cap or the eyes of conjunctivitis. We ponder the effects of a glass of wine on breast milk or what kept the baby up squirming and crying until 3:00 o'clock this morning—the sushi or the wine? When will

we get to lay our head on a pillow for six blessed hours in a row? How long will it be until we can really enjoy an evening out? In addition to the sheer volume of tasks, having an infant is like walking into a wonderland of strange and conflicting information. Trying to decipher it all while the days are packed with time-sensitive details feels daunting, especially when we're tuckered out by our own lack of sleep. It is easy to feel like we're drowning in responsibilities.

I want to say, dear Mom, please go easy on yourself! God did not give you this precious child to make you crazy. Rather, our Savior promises to be with us, giving us the strength and help we need for each day. Repeatedly, God's Word reminds us to live without fear . . . which includes dropping the fear of failure as a mom. Proverbs 3:24 says, "When you lie down, you will not be afraid; when you lie down, your sleep will be sweet." And in Mark 5:36, Jesus says, "Don't be afraid; just believe." He invites us to cling to Him in our hearts as we face challenges that push us beyond the comfort of our lives before baby, and the help God provides may come in ways that we never expected.

Sometimes, God's provision comes through a friend who is experiencing her own struggles as a new mom, or perhaps God encourages us by a phone call from someone far away, even if we are the one to reach out and make the call. If you are like me, it might be a good idea to just pack up Baby and take a walk outdoors to clear the mind and behold the grandeur that God gives us in nature. Thanking Him for the beauty of trees and flowers or for the brilliance of cardinals against a backdrop of snow can lift spirits on days when stress weighs us down. We do not walk alone; God is with us all the time, even when we do not sense His presence. And let's not forget that when we look for Him, we will find Him just as He promises. You may see God in the sunset, through the smile on a neighbor's face, or perhaps through deep peace in your heart as a breeze rustles leaves overhead, causing our baby to look up in wonder.

Better Together

If one part suffers, every part suffers with it;
if one part is honored, every part rejoices with it.

If someone invites you to share in the birth of her baby, do not miss it for anything! If you must rearrange your life to attend, do it. You will always be glad you did. The beginning of life is sacred, and so is the end, as I learned, holding my mother's hand while she slipped from this world into the next. I remember how thrilled I was by my niece's invitation to be with her for her first baby's arrival. Unlike my previous personal experience, this time we anticipated a birth—the first for this generation of our family, and I felt honored.

My daughter and I were both asked to share in the birth of Alyssa's baby. We tried to keep our schedules fluid, since none of us could guess when the little one would make his or her entrance, but we had out-of-town company for Mother's Day weekend, and I promised to serve brunch for my mother-in-law and the rest of the family. However, a phone call late on Saturday afternoon changed our plans in a minute. Alyssa was in active labor, which propelled Johanna and me off to the hospital three hours away. When we entered the birthing room, it was obvious that Alyssa was hard at work. She looked beautiful, squatting on a yoga ball, in a plaid shirt she wears for horseback riding. Her family circled around, taking turns massaging her back, offering ice chips, and holding her hands. She didn't need any more helpers, but as her aunt and cousin, we stepped quietly into the room that felt like holy ground. We didn't want to be in the way; we just wanted to offer comfort and support in any way we could.

Alyssa labored like a champ, riding out each contraction with focused determination. She followed every suggestion offered by nurses and her doctor. All night the contractions gripped her with pain while the long strip of monitor paper spewed forth its undulating line indicating contractions coming longer, stronger, and closer together. We helped her breathe, change positions, and get in and out of a bathtub. Her mom rubbed her feet while someone else pressed on her back and hips.

Through the window we watched the moon rise bright and full over Lake Superior.

This is how we passed the night—taking turns assisting—while Alyssa did all the hard, painful work of labor. Time seemed to stand still in the birthing room, but eventually the sky grew lighter over the lake, and the sun crept up, promising a bright blue-skied day. In the morning, Alyssa's doctor checked her progress and reported the news that after laboring diligently without meds for twenty-four hours, Alyssa was at a whopping five centimeters . . . only half way there.

It was time for an epidural so she could rest and gain strength for pushing. A wonderful anesthesiologist worked his magic, relieving the agony of contractions. Alyssa slept while her body continued to labor on its own. This was a great relief for her and for the rest of us who watched her suffer long enough. When suddenly it was time for Alyssa to push, each of us jumped to help as we could. Two people held her legs, someone ran for more ice chips, and with a wet washcloth, we wiped her brow. She had pushed hard for well over an hour when we started to see the baby's head. This is the precious moment when I think the angels stand by holding their breath, waiting with us to see the baby safely delivered.

Oskar Lewis arrived—a perfect nine pounds, nine-and-a-half ounces with bright eyes that looked straight at his mama! We wept, we laughed, and we sang praises to God for this beautiful child. Alyssa's dad stepped in and read from Psalm 139. "For you created my inmost being; you knit me together in my mother's womb. I praise you because I am fearfully and wonderfully made; your works are wonderful, I know that full well. My frame was not hidden from you when I was made in the secret place, when I was woven together in the depths of the earth. Your eyes saw my unformed body." (Psalm 139:13-16,) Alyssa held her son on her chest with tears of relief streaming down her cheeks, love pouring and rushing from her to him while he squawked in her face. Then he settled in to nurse. Such love is the love of a family and a mother's affection for her child. Baby Oskar was born into a circle of love on Mother's Day. What a privilege to share in this high moment of my niece's life.

While Alyssa knew we could not take away the pain of her labor, she understood that as frail people, we are stronger together. I appreciate how willing she was to welcome us into the messy awkwardness of bringing a baby into the world. She was not overly concerned about her privacy or comfort. Rather, she humbled herself and invited us to share this life-changing experience.

How often in life do we attempt to face trials all by ourselves? Perhaps it's out of pride or because we don't want to bother someone else, but what a worthwhile connection grows when we share challenging times with loved ones. We are strengthened by walking with others—not alone—and those who are invited to walk by our side, perhaps while holding our hand or simply offering ice chips, are enormously blessed as well.

Oskar Lewis

Go with Your Gut!

Do not forsake wisdom, and she will protect you;
love her, and she will watch over you.
The beginning of wisdom is this: Get wisdom.
Though it cost all you have, get understanding.

PROVERBS 4:6-7, NIV

We've all been in that place where we are so glad to know another mom whose baby is the same age as ours. Each of us needs a friend who shares the challenges of mothering on a daily basis. Then one day, a get-together at her house makes it evident that the two of you do this mothering thing very differently. It might be your philosophy to keep your home much the same as it was before baby, whereas your friend has completely changed her home to be a safe baby-haven where anything that could possibly be considered dangerous has been removed. The living area looks more like a professional daycare. Couples' dinners in the dining room will not be happening at this home for at least several years, as changing table, baby swing, pack-n-play, and baby-gym have taken over. Numerous gates, outlet covers, and cabinet latches tell you right away which mom is going to win an award for the safest house in the neighborhood! Sure, you might put a lock on the cabinet under the kitchen sink, but plants, books, and candlesticks still decorate the coffee table.

Previously, you felt comfortable with your laid-back approach to readying your home for baby, but seeing another's style makes it easy to doubt your own. Is a trip to the baby store for a few more gadgets necessary? Do I fail as a mom who cares for her child's well-being? Is my friend judging my relaxed style of parenting? Am I judging her extra vigilance?

Home safety is just one area where our common sense may look different from a friend's. Some parents urge their babies to develop skills as fast as possible. Reading readiness cannot come soon enough, and some new moms see the value of baby sign language. The whole question of breastfeeding versus formula is a big topic, and just like each mom had different preferences, so does each baby. In every case, we mother our young based on our own experience and personal wisdom. We each take advice and apply it in our own way by keeping what works and tossing the rest. And guess what, Moms . . . this is a good thing!

I'll never forget the barrage of advice I received at a shower for our second baby. I must have appeared very green at mothering, since each guest was instructed to offer a piece of insight while I opened gifts. I was buried in well-intentioned wisdom that was not my own, and my head spun with feelings of inadequacy. I felt sure I could never follow each person's advice, and truly, I could not, especially since much of it was conflicting. However, there was one mother's words that rang true and stuck with me through the years. Stella, whose children were older and for whom I held immense respect, saw my distress and came to my rescue. She pulled me aside, gave me a hug, and whispered in my ear, "Don't let all this advice worry you. Keep for yourself only what feels absolutely right for you and forget the rest!" Her words of wisdom freed me, and I laughed as she let me go.

There is such a thing as mother's intuition, a God-given ability to know our baby and apply the common sense that God builds into each of us. He promises us wisdom when we ask for it. He gives us good minds to process another's logic and to practice what seems best. We may not mother our children just like our friends, but as we seek to be discerning moms, we need to be free to go with our gut about what works well for us and our baby.

Mom—
Hero in the Night

On my bed I remember you; I think of you
through the watches of the night.
Because you are my help, I sing in the shadow
of your wings. My soul clings to you;
your right hand upholds me.

PSALM 63:6-8, NIV

As the mother of an infant, you may have experienced a night like the one my friend described a few years back. At 3:00 a.m. she and her husband were awakened by the cries of their son. Her wise husband quickly brokered a deal by offering to get out of bed and feed the baby if she would cover the day-care drop on her way to work. With their agreement in place, he climbed out of bed, warmed some milk, and fed their son a small bottle to settle him back into his crib. Just as mom and dad dozed off, their son urgently communicated his displeasure with such a meager meal.

Keri sighed an audible "mother knows best" sigh as she left the bedroom to gather up her son to further sustain his recent growth spurt. She warmed a full-size bottle and collapsed downstairs on the couch with her baby sprawled on her chest. At a moment like this, it's easy to feel frustrated that as a mom you are usually the parent who successfully problem solves during the wee hours of the morning, and your husband may not be the only one who gets up and goes to work all day. In fact, you wouldn't be the first mother to have feelings of anger or self-pity while stumbling in exhaustion to care for your infant at night.

Under a tent of blankets, this mom and baby kept warm. Keri closed her eyes and listened to the rhythmic sucking sounds of her son, who obviously found great pleasure in his bigger bottle. Suck. Swallow. Suck. Swallow. The pattern calmed her heart, and what came next split through her frustrated exhaustion. Her baby suddenly stopped drinking and flipped up the blanket so he could see his mom's face directly in front of his own. Then he grinned a wide, milky, three-tooth grin. She couldn't help but smile back in pleasure, while Peter returned to his meal. Several times as he happily consumed his bottle, he stopped to lock eyes with his mom, smile, and then contentedly return to drinking his milk.

When the clock struck 4:00 a.m., Keri realized she had been enjoying her son for almost an hour. If she hadn't gotten up with him, she would have missed the most beautiful part of the new day. She breathed prayers for Peter and offered thanks for this special time to feed him, even if it did cost her precious sleep. She prayed for her husband who works hard. She thought about how grateful she is for their life together. She prayed for energy to get through her day at the office, and she thanked God for blessing her with baby Peter, who completely stole her heart.

As she climbed back into bed to catch a little more rest before the alarm sounded, she whispered to her husband that the baby was satisfied and so was she. She also mentioned that it would be his turn to take Peter to day-care.

My Weakness Is His Strength

[Jesus] said to me, "My grace is sufficient for you,
for my power is made perfect in weakness."
Therefore I will boast all the more gladly about
my weaknesses, so that Christ's power may rest on me.

2 CORINTHIANS 12:9, NIV

Some days you might feel quite sure that your mommy license could be revoked at any moment! What will it take? One more terrible episode that lands you at Urgent Care explaining every little nick and scratch that mars your baby's skin? None of us can stand seeing our little one in pain, but how much worse we feel when we have been the one to accidentally inflict a hurt.

It didn't take long for me to learn that I should not clip our newborn's tiny fingernails. At less than one week of age, she gouged her smooth pink baby cheeks with her flailing razor-nails, so I attempted to prevent more cuts by clipping them. Have you ever given a mouse a manicure? It's just as tricky! For as careful as I tried to be—steadying her itty-bitty fingers in mine—I accidentally drew blood, making her scream in pain. Immediately, I handed her to my husband and ran out of the room like a chicken, and that little episode was only the first of my many mother-blunders.

While I am at it, let me add that I'm not proud to admit that while zipping our baby into her one-piece sleeper, I caught some skin. Another bad day: I left a partially opened pineapple can where our fruit-loving baby could reach it . . . and it deeply sliced his finger. And who hasn't cut a little ear when a wiggling toddler refuses to sit still for a haircut? These humbling experiences cause me to shudder. What was I thinking?

On another occasion, our two little pumpkins were dressed and ready for church the day we were to stand up front and become members. The only thing I needed was a clean cloth diaper from the dryer in the basement. I set baby Bjorn down in his infant seat next to his nineteen-month old sister and made a mad dash to the basement, pushing the door closed behind me. Apparently, it was almost closed, because the next thing I heard was clattering and yelping as both babies tumbled the entire flight of stairs in a frightening blur of hands, feet, and heads. In horror, I heard their noisy descent and flung a pile of clean laundry to cushion the landing—a nanosecond too late, however. All I accomplished was piling diapers on top of them.

An amazing number of terrifying thoughts runs through a mom's mind between that awful moment of impact and the first unsettling shrieks. You dread the cries, but you also know they are a sure sign of survival; you hold your breath, imagining Child Protective Services at your door as you look for blood. I scooped those pitiful babes into my trembling arms to comfort their undone spirits as I carried them upstairs. When their cries subsided, I ran next door to my wonderful neighbor, Nurse Debbie. Together we felt clavicles, arms, legs, and examined pupils and heads. Everybody was intact—everyone except for me. I was terribly shaken.

You see, on Sunday mornings I am alone. My husband is a pastor and goes to church a couple hours early, so this is my time to appreciate what single moms do every day and, obviously, do it better than me. Hats off to you women who live every day in this manner. You have my utmost admiration and respect! I am lousy at flying solo, especially when we're all supposed to be neatly dressed and delivered on time, and I swear the devil works overtime on Sunday mornings.

We didn't make it to church that day. I found that sitting on my neighbor's front porch to be far more consoling than even my favorite song at church. I held my bruised little ones and wondered how else I would screw up in the years to come. All the while, Debbie calmly reminded me that God builds babies to be tough. I felt weak in my mom-skills, so how fortunate for me and for all mothers that God's grace is sufficient. His power is most evident when we are weak (2 Corinthians 12:9).

Unconditional Love of Rabbit

See what great love the Father has lavished on us,
that we should be called children of God!
And that is what we are!

1 JOHN 3:1, NIV

As parents, we have great influence over the lives of our little ones. We choose their name, what they eat, where they sleep, and who gets to hold them. We pick their pediatrician, car seat, type of diapers, and for the moment, we get to dress them in whatever adorable outfit strikes our fancy. This is our prerogative, since babies are completely dependent, but considering the intense helplessness of newborns, it's amazing how capable they are of expressing opinions at a very tender age.

Babies have definite likes and dislikes from the get-go, and they communicate their feelings loudly. Some babies enjoy being snugly swaddled, while other's like to pull their hands free. One baby discovers his thumb is a wonderful digit to suck, while another prefers three fingers. Some babies demand to be held by Mom, and some will relax in the arms of anyone who is warm and breathing. When it comes to the best-loved toy that is favored over all others, the baby chooses.

When our baby Karl-Jon made his choice, he never wavered. For whatever reason, he fell headlong in love with his Goodnight Moon rabbit with blue-and-white stripes and a soft gray face. Karl-Jon and his buddy "Rabbit" (pronounced "wabbit") were inseparable. Wherever Karl-Jon went, Rabbit went, be it on stroller walks to the park, to play in the sandbox, to friends' homes, or to bed. Rabbit was propped next to Karl-Jon at tea parties or whenever we read books together. Rabbit was an easy companion, who—thank goodness—tolerated occasional "swimming sessions" in the wash machine.

Despite all the love he received, Rabbit led a treacherous life. One day he went missing from the church nursery, and our almost-one-year-old was distraught. Many desperate phone calls and search parties attempted to recover the lost bunny, but to no avail. While it seemed too extravagant, we purchased another Goodnight Moon rabbit, and the love affair continued with its beautiful unconditional nature. Peace was restored to our home, much to everyone's relief.

Some months later, during suppertime, Rabbit sat perched on the high chair tray, dangerously close to a plate of spaghetti. To avoid a tomato-stained Rabbit, I picked him up and placed him on the stove so he could watch us from a safe distance. Suddenly, my error was apparent when during dinner, the back of Rabbit's leg began to smolder. I left the burner on. Oops. Hastily, I grabbed Rabbit and doused him under the faucet as the gravity of the situation registered as a catastrophe for Karl-Jon and his concerned siblings. We did our best to soothe our son, and when Rabbit dried out, I gave his leg more stuffing and a polka-dot patch that contrasted nicely with his stripes. Karl-Jon didn't mind the patch. At bedtime he fiddled with the patch with his fingers, kissed it, and affectionately proclaimed, "Wabbit all better, Mommy."

That wasn't the end of Rabbit's calamitous adventures (why is the most-loved toy also the most accident prone?). One day, Karl-Jon innocently stood at our front door watching a magnificent snow fall. Suddenly, out of nowhere, bounded a huge husky who nosed open the door and boldly snatched Rabbit from our stunned toddler's hands. Off the dog frolicked and so did Rabbit, bunny ears and tail bouncing up and down with every leap. Karl-Jon dissolved into shrieks of distress while I pulled on shoes and chased the dog with all my strength. Naturally, the husky loved the game of "keep-away-as-frantic-mom-tries-to-recover-dumb-bunny." My neighbor happened to look out and witness this tragedy in the making. She quickly grabbed a coat and dashed out her door, leaping with me around trees and over heaps of snow trying to corner the pup and rescue Rabbit. At last we did, but not until we were panting and laughing at our ridiculous predicament. I gratefully carried the dog-slobbered Rabbit back to Karl-Jon, who hugged him with all his might. Dog mangled, spaghetti stained, rain-soaked, or full of ice cream—that rabbit received unconditional love from the little boy who treasures him to this day.

As I looked at Rabbit with his battered body and dangling, sweet head (listing to the left), it struck me that as moms, we sometimes feel just as worn out and stained. Some days we wear the perfume of sour baby puke while the circles under our eyes tell the truth of sleep deprivation. We might feel squidgy around the middle, painfully aware that all the coconut butter in the world will not erase stretch marks. And that's just the outside.

The inside isn't all that attractive either. I know I can be snappish when provoked, and I can let envy drown out contentment. I've been ungrateful, resentful, and downright selfish. It will take more than a polka-dot patch to heal all my sinful ways, but like Rabbit, I am still loved. Not only am I loved by my child, but I am loved unconditionally by my Heavenly Father who sees past the blemishes of body and mind. Love covers a multitude of sin so thoroughly that it can drown out the darkness in our souls and replace it with blazing light.

In the goodness of God's patience and grace, I am encouraged to know that His love gives me hope I can count on. I dig deep and find a remnant of joy and zest, even when the mirror tells me I need a rest and I don't know when that is practically going to happen. Even as I am spilled on, worn out—at the end of my energy—I cling to the love that God offers unconditionally. I can't earn it, I don't deserve it, but I totally depend on it.

Food for Thought

I am the vine; you are the branches.
If you remain in me and I in you, you will bear much fruit;
apart from me you can do nothing.

JOHN 15:5, NIV

Does the amount of time spent feeding your infant ever amaze you? Whether you are breastfeeding or offering a bottle, newborns need to eat eight to twelve times a day, seven days a week. At forty-five to fifty minutes per feeding (not to mention the time it takes to change a diaper and soothe the little eater back to sleep), mothers of newborns assume this unrelenting task that requires more hours than a full-time job. Fit that together with the other demands of the day, and now you see how mothers of newborns are busy women who barely find time to eat their own meals because keeping the baby well-fed is the highest priority.

The huge amount of time spent nourishing a baby is a mixed bag for us moms. On a positive note, being the main feeder allows us to sit down and put our feet up.

Face it—sometimes it's the only rest we get. Plus, we can make the most of the opportunity to cuddle and connect with our infant. Feeding allows us time to take in the wondrous beauty of our baby. It's our chance to luxuriate in the wonder of the intimate bond between baby and mom, one feeding at a time. In our lap, we hold a little person whose sense of security grows more solid with every offering of sustenance.

The challenge of this great responsibility is its time-consuming nature. As you know, fitting all the feedings around everything else is tricky. Especially if your baby joins older siblings, is a twin, or a triplet. "Busy" doesn't begin to describe the challenge of your schedule. Still, feeding a baby is so important, we take the time or make the time, sometimes sacrificing much to make it happen. God wired mothers to never forget to feed their baby, but what might slip our mind is that moms also get hungry, and I'm not talking about craving a perfect cobb salad and ginger tea. Just as our infant thrives on physical food to grow a strong body, and on skin-to-skin contact to gain a sense of security, our connection with God is necessary to ground our life in Him.

Jesus said, "I am the vine; you are the branches. If you remain in me and I in you, you will bear much fruit; apart from me you can do nothing (John 15:5). In a sense, we are much like a human baby whose life and security come from the all-important connection with its mother. The relationship that helps us grow is with the ultimate giver of life, Jesus Christ. Out of that relationship we find security that encourages us to be spiritually productive and become "fruit-bearers."

As we are sequestered with our babe, feeding away while the clock ticks on, let us remember that our task is not only important, it's a privilege of ours for a finite amount of time. When it's your turn to feed, savor the time as a chance to sit down, take it easy, and enjoy these special moments with your baby. Maybe this is your only chance to pick up the Bible or another book and read for a little while. By doing so, you and your baby both receive nourishment.

Meditating on a piece of scripture while you nurse or give a bottle is a great way to utilize this time. As we lovingly stroke our baby's head, let us see our action as an example of our great need to remain close to God.

God's Plans Might Not Look Like Ours

"For I know the plans I have for you," declares the LORD,
"plans to prosper you and not to harm you,
plans to give you a hope and a future."

JEREMIAH 29:11, NIV

These are the words given to the Israelites while they were exiles in Babylon. As depressed refugees waiting in a foreign country, the prophet Jeremiah encouraged them to look beyond their present situation. As improbable as it seemed, he offered assurance that God had a plan for them that included a bright future. Jeremiah insisted that the Israelites needed to pray earnestly and hold fast to their faith. He wanted them to know that God promised to hear their prayers and would not let them down.

As the mom of a newborn, have you ever felt like an exile in the foreign land of motherhood? It takes a lot of effort to reshape our lives to accommodate a new baby and his or her needs. So much in our personal world is altered, and it's easy to worry about what lies ahead for our family and especially for our newborn infant. This world doesn't seem like a very hospitable place, especially for a person so tiny and helpless as our baby, but we can let God's loving words of hope comfort our soul. As we pray for our baby, it's okay to ask God to give our child a good start in life that leads to a bright future.

It may seem impossible, but God loves our baby even more than we do. Yes, I know we moms love our little ones with our entire being, but God's love outpaces ours, and as God loves us, He wants us to love Him in return. This is the essence of faith. It means believing that God really does love our child more completely than we do, so we trust Him with our baby's life. No matter how crazy or difficult that may be, this is the greatest struggle any mother faces, and it means believing that God knows what's best for our child.

While Scripture says that God's plan is for prosperity, His plan might look completely different from the world's standard for wealth and success. Our prayers do not guarantee a brilliant student or even an average one;

rather, it means aligning our will to that of our Heavenly Father. We want for our child what God would choose for him or her. Yes, we pray for protection for our young child along with sound health and a great education too, but as we allow God to have His way in our baby's life, we gain a growing, vibrant faith that draws us ever closer to God. Being close to God means we are blessed by a life rooted in peace.

Baby Hair

"And even the very hairs
of your head are numbered."

MATTHEW 10:30, NIV

What could be softer or invite tender caresses more than the top of our infant's head? As we hold our baby close, or carry them in a front pack, inhaling the sweet fragrance of their fuzzy little head, we can't help kissing it, loving its round shape and the gentle slope that leads to the baby's neck and shoulders. We study every detail—every little shock of hair, each ear-fold, and infant birthmark that make our little one unique.

Some infants arrive with a "Beatle wig," thick and dark, waiting for the rest of the baby's body to catch up. Others surprise us with a hairless scalp that resembles a polished bocce ball. I birthed one baby boy with blonde hair that turned dark brown and another that did the exact opposite. Some babies sport fine wisps, while others are born with generous mounds of springy ringlets.

Whatever type of hair decorates your baby's head, know that it was chosen by God as part of His creative design for your child.

Not only did God dream up the kind of hair each person sports, He knows the exact number of hairs that cover each head. You may think this is inconsequential, but in the book of Matthew, Jesus mentions this detail to his closest friends as He sends them out to do good work in His name. Sharing His knowledge of their hair-count is simply His way of saying He knows them intimately, and therefore they need not fear. The "do not be afraid" message is a recurring theme in the Bible, proving that we tend to be fearful folks who need lots of reassurance.

Obviously, there is a lot to fear in this world, and with a new baby, our concerns for the future tend to grow. We can't help considering the condition of our planet—relationally, environmentally, and spiritually. In what kind of world will our child grow up? Will it be safe enough? Economically productive enough? Will it provide a good education? While our hearts may naturally run toward fear, this is a great time to focus our thoughts on God who made us, who cares for us, and who loves our baby even more capably than we are able to do ourselves. God is aware of the trivia of our lives. He knows the very number of hairs on our heads, and He is familiar with all our fears.

Just as one day we feel awed by our infant's perfect head and strengthening neck muscles, on another we might shudder at our baby's vulnerability when we see the heartbeat pulsing through the soft spot on top of the head. As moms, we are tuned into our baby's tenacity and helplessness—their strength and incredible dependence. I have a hunch it's not that different from the way God sees us. Sometimes, we are weighed down by fears and vulnerabilities (real or imagined), and sometimes we stand strong. Either way He finds us, and His heart is moved with compassion and love. As we carry our babies, they carry us, helping us grow less fearful and more confident in God's love.

Sounds that Surround

Whatever is true, whatever is noble, whatever is right,
whatever is pure, whatever is lovely,
whatever is admirable—if anything is excellent
or praiseworthy—think about such things.

PHILIPPIANS 4:8, NIV

For a baby's ears, what an incredible shock birth must be. Before this point, his womb-world is bathed in the soft whirring of blood flow, the comforting beat of his mother's heart, and entertaining gurgles of digestion. Babies hear sounds from the outside world as well, but these are muffled and indistinct, sort of the way we hear when our heads are under water. But at birth, bright lights and startling sounds tell a newborn they have entered a completely new realm.

A newborn's auditory nerves are piqued by all sorts of sounds—alarms, strange voices, laughing, monitors beeping, footsteps, phones ringing, and doors closing. It's always reassuring to see a baby respond to sound, and

it's also amazing what they can sleep through. How about when we bring our baby home? To what sounds will they become accustomed? Will they hear siblings' chatter, birds chirping, a dog barking, music playing, traffic, water running, or voices that they knew before they were born? Will sounds give them comfort or do the opposite?

Our daughter has a melody that dances in her head. One day as she hummed it, I asked what she was singing. She said she didn't know, but it's a melody that has always been familiar, though she wasn't sure why. I did a little digging, and we realized it's from Franz Schubert's Fifth Symphony—a piece we played over and over before she was born as well as when she was an infant—and there it holds fast, ingrained in her mind's ear to stay.

When we consider the sensitivity of a baby's ears and the strong connection between what we hear and emotions, let's contemplate the sounds that fill our

homes. Will our newborn hear voices raised in anger or be soothed by loving tones? Will they fall asleep to gentle music or sense joy in the sounds of heartfelt laughter? As babies quickly grow into toddlers and toddlers into children, remember they are mightily influenced by everything they hear from the very beginning. Be mindful of surrounding your little one with whatever is pure, whatever is lovely, whatever is admirable—filling them with good sounds on which to grow up. Like the tune that remains in our daughter's auditory memory, the sounds of babyhood influence us for many years to come.

In the Nick of Time

Therefore, do not worry about tomorrow,
for tomorrow will worry about itself.
Each day has enough trouble of its own.

MATTHEW 6:34, NIV

Raising a baby is a constantly changing process because babies are a dynamic bunch. Trying to keep up with their speedy development is a challenge. If you receive an adorable peanut-sized romper that says "three months" on the tag, wash it immediately and slide your newborn in. Even if it swallows too much of your tiny babe, don't be tempted to tuck it away thinking you'll pull it out at three months. It's very likely that your baby will zoom past the suggested age, and never get to wear Aunt Krissy's lovely gift. These little buggers grow faster than mushrooms in a damp basement.

In addition to expanding girth and height, our babies fly through various developmental stages that keep us on our toes. As any traveling parent will say upon return-ing home, every week of growth for a baby produces huge changes. One minute we're holding an infant with a bobblehead that lags behind its moving torso, kaleidoscope eyes roll in unfocused circles, and about ten minutes later we tote a sturdy-necked child who turns toward sounds and knows our face.

Ultimately, this is good. God made babies to grow quickly, but the challenge is to keep pace as our baby charges upward to the next size of clothes and the subsequent slot on the chart of developmental tasks. Just when we begin to understand one stage, they leapfrog to the next. This might mean that the baby, who at one week learned to crawl, suddenly hurtles his little body out of the crib in the middle of the night. This is hard on unsuspecting parents who didn't think their baby was capable of such gymnastics.

Even as we worry that we may not know what to do at each stage, we seem to be given what we need for each day. This is the miracle that amazes me. With a newborn, I worried that I wouldn't know how to handle a one-year-old. Then suddenly we had an eighteen-month-old plus a newborn, and bingo, the next year our third arrived, pushing me dangerously close to insanity. Somehow, though, God—through His grace—gets us through, providing what we need often in the last screeching moment. We understand a six-month-old best when we have one, and then when the teething or the colic is over, our expertise fades and we wonder with puzzlement how we knew what to do with a six-month-old.

This is one of the greatest wonders of being a mother. It urges us to believe that we don't have to worry about tomorrow because tomorrow will come complete with concerns of its own. I'd like to add that because of our Heavenly Father, it will surely come with all the grace, wisdom, knowledge, and understanding that is required for that day as well. Take a deep breath, Mom, and don't worry that you don't know what to do when kindergarten comes. When you have a kindergartener, you'll know. And even more amazing than that, when you must look up to make eye contact with a teenager, God will surprise you with oodles of wisdom and whatever else you need for that season. It will happen in the nick of time, and more than likely, not a moment before.

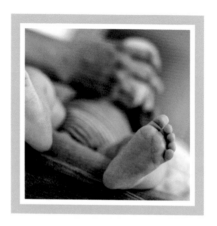

You Make a Terrible Mother!

Love is patient, love is kind.

1 CORINTHIANS 13:4, NIV

After five years straight of living with a pregnant or breastfeeding wife, my patient husband's patience was wearing thin. I can't really blame him. He went to bed for hundreds of nights with a whale of a wife, and once the newborn arrived, he went to bed alone while I rocked and nursed the baby down the hall. When we had our third and final baby, I savored the waning precious night feedings while my husband appreciated them less and less. By the time our infant son was seven months old, I should not have been surprised to discover that the good daddy in our house was feeding our baby a bottle before I had a chance to sit down and nurse him. Eric says he didn't mean to sabotage breastfeeding but aimed to streamline the bedtime routine and give me a break. It did not matter; it was sabotage to me. When I finally realized why our baby boy refused me, I vehemently informed my husband, "You make a terrible mother!"

I'm not proud to report that I occasionally repeated this statement at certain moments when I felt it was deserved. You know, like when you're horrified to discover that your baby has been out in the cold woods for hours without a hat or mittens, or when the pacifier has been dragged through a dish of chocolate ice cream on the way to the baby's mouth. I don't mean to devalue my husband's parenting skills, but there is a certain set of rules that applies particularly to moms. Dads just weren't meant to have a mother's intuition.

My husband is the father, designed with other gifts that fulfill different needs for babies. He saw things I completely missed, like car seats that need tighter straps and smoke detectors that blink for fresh batteries. He brings music into the house and builds a fence around the yard, providing safety and freedom for the babies and peace of mind for me. These fathering attributes are not to be overlooked or underappreciated.

The truth is, for the few times I've pointed my finger and yelled, "You make a terrible mother," there are many more situations that prove I'd flunk at fatherhood. Could it be that God in His wisdom provides for the care and welfare of babies through moms and dads . . . and even older siblings, aunts, uncles, friends, and grandparents? While we moms might think our intuition is the ultimate force that protects our young, we can learn a lot from others who also care for our baby, extending the family of love that encircles our child. When we are patient and kind toward our spouse and with others who love our offspring, everyone wins, especially our beloved baby, who thrives best in an atmosphere of peace.

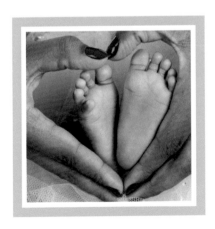

From the
Lips of Infants...

From the lips of infants and children
you have ordained praise . . .

PSALM 8:2, NIV

One day while driving home from a trip to the country, my friend took her favorite shortcut through a small Michigan town as she was in a hurry to get home. Suddenly, in front of her loomed a sign that read "Bridge Out." She simultaneously hit the breaks and uttered a startled "Oh shit!" Two seconds later, from the back seat floated the sweet voice of her extremely verbal baby girl who repeated, "Oh shit!" followed by a quizzical, "Oh shit . . . what that, Mommy?" While the frustration of knowing she would arrive home late trounced this mom's last nerve, so did this honest question from her tiny talker who was eager to build her vocabulary.

If some version of this tale sounds familiar to you, you know how it feels to be chastened by a baby whose simplicity and innocence cause you to pause and consider what you said. If you're like me, you replay the scene and wonder next time, could I possibly keep my exclamation confined to my head? Better yet, decide to just clean up the vocabulary and start over with greater determination. While contemplating a fair response to our little ones' questions, we mostly hope they will not retain our "colorful" spontaneity for instant recall at Grandma's house or church.

At some point, it becomes apparent that babies are sponges built with the ability to quote us word-for-word. So, we must be okay with what they say because we said it first. It's that simple. Even before a baby utters their first words, they are listening—always listening—and learning everything they hear. At first, it's just sounds, but before long we see how eager they are to attach meaning to each sound. Their minds are beautiful blank slates, ready to record words from our lips; therefore, every crass utterance and scrawl expression enter their heads, tarnishing their clean slates, and circles to exit their mouths complete with inflection that matches ours to a tee.

This crazy phenomenon illustrates how we influence our offspring, while on the other hand, when we hear our words spoken by a son or daughter, we become humbly aware of their influence on us. Knowing that our sweet baby copies us, right down to the tone of our voice, we listen more carefully to our own blathering. Do our words bless or curse? Do they build up or break down? Do we sound frantic or peaceful? Fearful or thankful? Sarcastic or encouraging?

The Psalmist writes, "From the lips of infants and children you have ordained praise," declaring that even babies offer praise to God by what they say. Considering that newborns don't clearly enunciate, perhaps their cooing and verbal hieroglyphics are expressions of praise in God's ears. As babies grow and accumulate new words each day, let us give them even greater means by which to offer praise. As we chatter within earshot of our little ones, let our words praise God, give blessing, show patience, name gratitude, and offer encouragement. As babies become toddlers and as toddlers grow into small children, they will bless all who have the pleasure of hearing their sweet words.

Good Moms Need a Good Rest!

But for me, it is good to be near God.
I have made the Lord GOD my refuge.

PSALM 73:28, NIV

This wonderful new baby may be stretching you so far that sometimes you feel sure you haven't got what it takes to be a good mom. There is not one of us with a new infant who hasn't felt that way at times. Our little "bundles of joy" can quickly—will—morph into bundles of frustration. They test mental and emotional endurance like nothing else, so exhaustion takes on new meaning as our little one, who needs us more than anyone, interrupts our sleep night after night.

It is easy to let our hearts feel overburdened by new responsibilities. Have you ever wondered how a person so tiny could generate an entire load of laundry every day? There are the hours spent feeding, comforting, cuddling, and changing diapers, and these tasks are added to all the others that were already in our job description before the baby came home.

It is easy to feel discouraged—to let our minds wander backward in time to simpler days before our lives were run by an infant who sometimes feels like a ball and chain. We fondly remember when we could go running without a baby jogger. Going out for lunch with a friend could happen spontaneously, and shopping without a newborn was succinct and fun. Just getting out of the house was easier. In fact, so was getting in and out of the shower and finding time to read. Our minds romanticize our pre-babydom.

Perhaps this has never happened to you, but I know it has for plenty of us. To make matters more complicated, there is the inevitable nagging guilt thrumming in our ear—good moms don't feel this way. Baloney! Some days, even the best mom feels discouraged and frustrated with an insatiable need to scream. Every good mom feels this, and it is okay.

If you have a friend or a husband who suggests helping take some of the load, but you're afraid to accept any help, stop right there! Before you keel over with weariness, let someone take over while you take a glorious nap. Even if no one offers, tell your husband, a sister, your mother, a friend, a trusted neighbor, the UPS man—whomever—that you need a nap or you might not be safe. Perhaps you should not involve the UPS man, but any one of the others would be happy to give you time to replenish your reserves.

And when your head finally hits the blessed pillow, imagine that now you're the child, curling up next to the Sovereign Lord, who in His love wishes to be near you, offering peace as you unwind. Take some deep breaths and lean on Jesus, who promises to draw near to us when we draw near to Him. Allow His Spirit to soothe your weary soul.

Baby Shots

As a mother comforts her child,
so I will comfort you . . .

Isaiah 66:13, NIV

Immunizations can certainly make a baby out of us parents. It pains most moms to tote an innocent newborn into the pediatrician's office knowing that shots will be part of the visit. Any sensitive parent feels like they're being unusually cruel as they brace for the cries and possible fever that might follow, yet we are doing what is best to keep our little ones healthy.

If you feel stressed because your baby will most likely endure over twenty shots by the time they are fifteen months old, you are not alone. The immunization schedule, established by the American Academy of Pediatrics, has us heading to the clinic for shots at two, four, six, nine, twelve, and fifteen months, and unfortunately, our clever babies become increasingly wise to the situation with each passing episode of needle sticks.

I don't claim to have any wonderfully freeing advice for us moms who have a harder time with immunizations than our babies do, but I would like to point out a couple of things. The first is that sometimes in life we must choose between the lesser of two evils. Even amid controversy regarding the pros and cons of immunizing, the goodness of protecting our babies from illnesses far outweighs the possibility of the immunization causing harm. Plus, momentary pain that a shot inflicts is extremely small compared to suffering with an illness like hemophilus influenzae or whooping cough.

But if you question the safety of immunizations, speak with your pediatrician. Ours explains that the privilege of being immunized is one of the best, safest, most important gifts that modern medicine offers our babies. We have no idea what it was like for parents to fear polio and other serious illnesses not so many years ago.

On the day your baby receives his or her shots, this is what to expect. Fortunately, health clinics are savvy and kind about the way immunizations are given. Two nurses may administer the vaccines at a time so that the sticks are over in a few seconds. They are also sensitive to the fact that an upset infant feels the greatest comfort in his or her parent's arms, so holding your baby during and immediately after the procedure helps. Now for the silver lining to the immunization cloud: after the shots are given, your baby may be cuddlier than ever.

When you get home, enjoy your baby, who just wants to snuggle! Your little one may be a little sleepy or perhaps feel flushed and fussy, but the most soothing place for them is being close to Mom or Dad. This is when we settle ourselves on the couch and cuddle without guilt, appreciating the amazing wonder of holding and comforting our precious little one. What a blessing that in easing our child's hurts, we too find comfort. While being immunized is a little stressful for the baby, remember that it's far harder on us moms, who take the pain of our little ones on ourselves.

Walk with a Friend

Rejoice with those who rejoice;
mourn with those who mourn.

ROMANS 12:15, NIV

The buddy system is as important for mothers of newborns as it is for kids who swim in a lake at summer camp. Every hour, the lifeguards blow their whistles, alerting swimmers to grab their buddy's hand and hold it high, proving that everyone is safe and accounted for. The same rule ought to apply for us moms! As we navigate the deep waters of early motherhood, we need friends with whom we can share mutual support and understanding.

Supportive relationships might look different for each of us, but for me it means having a friend to talk to every day, and one whom I can text any time of the night. It might just be a quick chat in the morning to see how each other slept or to report how often we were up to feed the baby. I've never had the luxury of my mom or a sister living close by, so sharing the daily challenges of new mommy-hood with a friend is important.

In the beginning, it was my friend Mindy who became my mothering buddy. She was on her second baby when I became pregnant with our first. Mindy shared with me a wealth of knowledge, introducing me to the confusing world of baby products and ways to get by using as few of these as possible. Mindy and I became great pals during daily conversations that ranged from a baby's ear infection to a recently read book. Mostly our talks offered much needed encouragement. Together we toted our kids to the beach, shared mugs of steaming tea in winter, and inhaled turtle sundaes in the summer. Another great bonus was the friendship that grew between our husbands.

When we had to move seven hundred miles away during our second pregnancy, the loss of my everyday friend was huge. But our new location in a Washington D.C. suburb didn't remain a lonely place for long. God provided new friends—two in particular—who shared the joys and sorrows of mothering with me.

The first time I bumped into Kerry was at church. It was her first Sunday, and my second. What a Godsend she was, bringing dinner two weeks later when our baby was born as if she had known me for years! To this day, she often senses what I need before I am aware of it myself.

Then one spring day, while chasing after my kids at our neighborhood park, I met a young mom who had a little boy the same age as one of mine, plus a beautiful baby girl in her arms. We struck up a conversation, and I learned that she was even newer to the neighborhood than me. Shelley let her humanity show immediately. She told me she felt nauseous, and asked if I had a plastic bag she could have in case she got sick on her walk home. What a great introduction, "Hi, it's nice to meet you . . . please don't mind if I throw up!" I liked her immediately. Her honest transparency let me know I could be myself with her. A lifelong friendship was born in a moment—one that enriches my life to this day.

Pregnancy and motherhood, each with their abundance of challenges, provide the soil in which strong bonds of friendship can grow. If we allow ourselves to be vulnerable and reach out to another mom who shares our struggles, our daily burdens feel lighter.

As an old Swedish proverb says, "Friendship doubles our joy and divides our grief." As you care for a new baby, don't try to do it alone. Find a friend who will walk with you through this strange new world of motherhood; then, on days when you feel defeated, it will be easy to call a friend and hear from someone you trust that everything is going to be okay. You will survive, and more joyfully so, when you walk with a friend.

In the Morning Light

Let the morning bring me word of your unfailing love;
for I have put my trust in you.
Show me the way I should go,
for to you I lift up my soul.

PSALM 143:8, NIV

As the mother of a young one, we don't often enjoy the privilege of an entire night of sleep. Do you remember the last time you went to bed at 10:00 p.m. and woke up feeling refreshed at 7:00 a.m.? I imagine it was many months ago. Now, on a good night we drag ourselves out of our warm nest to feed, diaper, feed some more, and return to bed without ever turning on the light, but some feedings just aren't that succinct. Baby Restless or Baby Colic can't seem to stop thrashing little legs, and you're certain there's nothing wrong with the lungs! You fear you'll wear out the rocking chair.

The problem with long nights spent alone in the company of a needy little human is that our minds can run amuck. For one thing, we are fighting exhaustion.

A tired person who sits up in complete darkness night after night must, on occasion, retrieve her mind from tricky rabbit trails that are riddled with gloom. These mental detours threaten to destroy our sense of security. Normal problems of the day grow larger and more complex under the cover of night. Sometimes, darkness envelops even the most optimistic mom.

When a fussy baby causes the night to seem endless and pitch-black loneliness closes in, it's natural to find our normal concerns looming larger than they have any business doing. Light is so important for our psyches. We need sunshine to lift our spirits and supply us with spirit-cheering vitamin D, but while we're propped up through inky hours, the light of morning feels far away. In addition to liberal amounts of vitamin D and plenty of dark chocolate, I have a favorite verse that has been my friend on many a long night. God led me to it on a bright and shining morning after a murky night fighting against the boogieman in my head. "Let the morning bring me word of your unfailing love; for I have put my trust in you. Show me the way I should go, for to you I lift up my soul" (Pslam 143:8).

Some nights we find ourselves at confusing crossroads needing to make difficult decisions. Other times, we feel overwhelmed by anxiety over the future. Unproductive worry flourishes mostly at night, which is why we need to arm ourselves with hopeful words from Scripture. Planting it in our mind allows us to repeat these encouraging words, reminding us that light exists at the end of the tunnel. The sun will come up tomorrow; there will be light in the morning. God will show me the way I should go. What could be more hopeful than to lift up our soul to the ever-loving, ever-caring God of the universe?

As a child, my grandmother told me with great confidence on a troubled night that "things will be better in the morning light." And she was right. As the new day dawned, the circumstances were the same, but as I opened my eyes to the morning light, I felt better prepared to cope.

Special Delivery

For you created my inmost being;
you knit me together in my mother's womb.

PSALM 139:13, NIV

What happens when your baby doesn't come any-where close to meeting the dreams that you have carried in your heart for this child? Perhaps you've just delivered a baby with Down syndrome, cerebral palsy, or some other serious life-altering condition.

It is completely understandable if your feelings vac-illate between shock and anger. Grieving is hard work that requires significant effort for parents in this situ-ation. In such a place of confusion and disappointment, our hearts ache as we struggle to let go of what might have been, and attempt to wrap our minds around what is. While this can be excruciating, the stories of "special needs" babies illustrate God's goodness in the most poi-gnant ways.

Laura was twenty-five years old when her son, Buddy, was born with Down syndrome. Laura's response in the face of what some might call a tragedy was anything but despair. She felt so excited and privileged to be the mother of such a special child. She remembers looking at her adorable son and thinking, "Wow, it's amazing that God is willing to trust us with one of his extra special babies." While she admits feeling concerned that she and her husband would be able to give Buddy all he would need, she also felt blessed to mother this amazing boy.

Perhaps Laura felt incredibly thankful for this particular son because only four years earlier she lost a baby at six and a half months. That heartbreaking loss may have been God's way of readying Laura's heart for the gift of Buddy. But that wasn't her only preparation. Laura remembers when she was seven, at Brownies; she had a soft spot for a friend with cerebral palsy. While the other girls in her troop seemed uncomfortable or even fearful, Laura enjoyed spending time with this extraordinary friend, drawing her into the troop's activities. When Buddy was born, Laura and her husband embraced the beautiful gift of their special baby.

They felt from the very beginning that he would be a powerful witness for God. They prayed that if one person could come to know God's love through their son, they would feel fulfilled in the special person God created him to be. And the truth of it is: God did create Buddy. He absolutely knit him together in his mother's womb. God made the inmost part of Buddy, as He did for each one of us. He makes the core of who we are, the part of us that loves, the part of us that will live forever. And God made Buddy according to His plan for his life.

When Buddy was a boy, he had a caregiver who worked with him to help develop strength and greater muscle flexibility. Through Buddy's loving heart and his joyful spirit, Buddy's therapist discovered the life-changing love of Jesus. Laura and her husband continue to celebrate the incredible ways that God uses their son, despite his handicaps, for God's goodness on this earth. Buddy is no disappointment. On the contrary, he is a remarkable person with an unusual ability to connect with others.

Gobsmacked!

Her children arise and call her blessed.

PROVERBS 31:28, NIV

A friend candidly told me that her first impression of mothering a newborn was to feel completely gobsmacked! (Okay, she is married to a Brit. Perhaps in the U.S. we would say flabbergasted.) This new mom never thought of herself as a selfish person, but suddenly she wondered. Like many mothers, she had worked hard to establish a career . . . then she had a baby. The abrupt change in role caused her to take a good hard look at herself. Suddenly, she could no longer order her world as she had before, and she felt utterly astounded by the way it made her feel.

As she anticipated the baby's arrival, she planned how her days would go. She thought she could impose her will and schedule on the baby to keep things running as efficiently as possible. What a shock when she realized that this tactic did not work. Suddenly, she didn't get to choose when to go to the bathroom or when to take a shower. She couldn't just pop on her running shoes and head out the door for a workout whenever the spirit moved. Worst of all, her baby demanded breastfeeding exclusively. Even if her husband offered a bottle that contained her milk, the baby went ballistic and screamed bloody murder.

For a person who is super organized and goes about her tasks with clockwork efficiency, the imposition of motherhood felt like, well . . . an imposition. No doubt, she wanted a baby, but the reality of relinquishing her desires for a succinct schedule began a journey of introspection. Could it be that this mom, like many of us, when we look closely at our motives, discover the self-centeredness that we dislike in our baby might be what we like least in ourselves? Might it also be God's plan to work self-ishness out of us by giving us an extremely needy little person whose care depends almost completely upon us?

Herein lies a wild mystery of motherhood. While the mother of an infant makes sacrifices for the goodness of her baby's life, she discovers a less self-centered version of herself that is better equipped to think of others' needs in many aspects of life. A surprising reality breaks through to moms who learn this simple lesson. We discover that greater joy lies in being thoughtful of others. Taking care of our own needs, on our own time—as good as that sounds—is not always the best thing for us. All of life is give-and-take. We give to others; we receive from others. For many years to come, we give a lot to our children, but in the dance of giving and receiving, we find deep fulfillment.

Recently, I attended the funeral of a woman, who, with her husband, lovingly raised seven children in a house no larger than 800 square feet. Mind you, this was many years before the "Tiny House Movement" made such quarters look romantic. Though she endured many difficult challenges through the years, she made sure that her family knew security born out of unconditional love. Her children spoke about their home that was filled with laughter and joy. She was known to remain calm and positive even in stressful situations. The natural selfishness that each of us is born with was worked out of her years ago, and because of that, her children gathered together and literally stood up and called her blessed. It was a beautiful sight to behold.

Moving Chaos

The LORD will keep you from all harm—
he will watch over your life; the LORD will watch
over your coming and going both now and forevermore.

PSALM 121:7-8, NIV

No matter which way our baby comes to us, through adoption or birth, there's a natural longing to take our baby home. Those of us with an infant who needs weeks or even months in a neonatal intensive care unit sense this desire most poignantly. When we finally get home with a new baby, however, we're suddenly aware that there's no nursery staff to fall back on, but we're glad that no one will pester us in the wee hours for a baby footprint or a blood draw. We settle in to make our own decisions and establish a routine that works for us. One decision we must make is when to venture out with our new baby.

For our family, the first outing looked very different for each of our babies. With our first, who was born during cold season in Michigan, I was okay with staying close to the nest where I could adjust to breastfeeding on my own couch. Only a few of our closest friends and my mom—a veteran nurse—were with us as we got acquainted with our newborn daughter. We were at home for two weeks before cabin fever drove us out of the house. Our first outing was to church, where baby Johanna was passed around—a different kind of communion—and survived it all just fine.

When it came to our second little one, just eighteen months later, it was a warm and golden September in Virginia, which felt more like summer. During the first week, we stretched out on blankets under giant oaks that surrounded our house, which gave Johanna a chance to chase butterflies and my husband and me time to relax and get to know our baby, Bjorn. Neighbors stopped by to admire him, and our garden seemed like a good place to adjust to life with two under the age of two. However, by the time number three arrived, it was springtime and we were raring to go. By day number four, with Johanna in the stroller, Bjorn in my husband's backpack, and Karl-Jon snuggled peacefully in my front pack, we headed off to Mount Vernon, where we could stroll between hedges of fragrant boxwood and enjoy the springtime foliage in the gardens. It was a warm spring afternoon and stands out as one of the happiest outings of my life. Karl-Jon didn't make a peep when we toured the house, and while our older two weren't ready for the guide's history lesson, they managed to remain quiet and stand still.

I felt a bit like a mother hen with my gaggle of chicks around me. Some folks commented on our bustling bunch, as we toted diaper bag, snacks, and water bottles. One older woman peered into my baby-pack and inquired about the age of our red-faced little cherub. I looked at my watch and answered in all honesty, "Four days, five hours," which in her opinion seemed like child abuse. "Take that baby home where he belongs!" she scolded with a fierce look on her face that meant business.

It did feel a tiny bit reckless to head out so soon after giving birth, but by number three, I felt great, and we were ready to roll. So, away from the worried woman we hurried, hoping she wouldn't follow. My husband and I gave each other a little smile, and on the way to our car, we began planning the next day's outing for a picnic along the Potomac and a stroll through the art museum. We were so delighted by our menagerie of moving chaos that nothing short of influenza could keep us home.

And why shouldn't we venture out? I have always loved Psalm 121, where God pays attention to our whereabouts. It says He watches our coming and going, both now and forevermore. I believe He literally knows exactly where we are, and what we are doing. This does not mean we are to live carelessly, or that God will tell us when to enjoy an outing or when to remain at home, but it does speak of God who lovingly cares about us as we move from place to place.

When our babies get older, and eventually make their way to the neighbors and someday to school, this verse feels even more pertinent. It calms my heart. As we commit our babies to Jesus's care time and again, no doubt they will mature and travel even farther from the nest. Whether your first outing with your baby feels appropriate at day four, or by week four, know that God surrounds you with His love, and leads you on your way.

Julia Child-less

Children are a heritage from the Lord,
offspring a reward from him.

PSALM 127:3, NIV

As soon as babies can utter a word, we teach them to say thank you. But what about us? Are we as diligent with our gratitude as we wish our children to be? Even on a terrible day, it's valuable to offer thanks for the many blessings we enjoy. Most importantly, we must not forget to thank God for the amazing gift of our new baby. Sometimes, we are so distracted by exhaustion, difficulties, or worry that we simply forget to give thanks for the baby who has come into our lives to become our family.

If you have watched the movie *Julie and Julia* you may recall the scene where Julia Child is standing in her kitchen in Paris when her husband, Paul, hands her a letter from her beloved sister, Dorothy. As she reads it, she begins to gasp at a particular piece of news. Emphatically and stoically she gasps, "Paul! Dorothy is pregnant!

Isn't that won-der-ful?!" And she truly means it. But the heartbreaking part of her statement comes not in her actual words, but in the fact that she can't say wonderful without breaking down in deep sobs. For years Julia and Paul had hoped to conceive, but they never do. While she is truly thrilled for her sister, her heart also aches for the baby that she and Paul will never have.

This scene puts tears in my eyes, reminding me that my children are a huge blessing from God—a gift from His hand—and when I see my children as such, my sense of pure gratefulness and joy in being their mother nearly explodes out of me.

Sure, there are sacrifices that all parents make, but being thankful is the best antidote to feeling sorry for oneself, especially when being a mom feels taxing. Of course, we fondly remember simpler days before baby. We may whine about the loss of spontaneous socializing that we used to enjoy. We may miss the money that paid for a movie and dinner. Diapers and nursing bras aren't glitzy or fun, but they are rather necessary to care for a newborn. We spend our money differently according to the new set of values that having a baby has set in place. As Psalm 127:3 states, "Children are a heritage from the LORD, offspring a reward from him." By this we are reminded what an incredible, beautiful, astounding gift a baby is. Whether your baby came by way of adoption, or natural birth, your baby is an extension of God's grace to you.

When our third pregnancy became apparent, I was in shock. I didn't know how I could handle three under three years and three weeks old, but God in His goodness was extra generous with us, as He provided plenty of energy, hand-me-downs, and even another car seat to smush into the back seat of our Volkswagen. He gave us trustworthy baby-sitters, extraordinary neighbors, and wonderfully loving surrogate grandparents who helped lighten our load.

Another provision was a little phrase that I liked to repeat for this newest baby whenever I tucked him into bed. I whispered in his ear, "You are a gift and a precious treasure from Jesus." I said this to remind myself that God would provide all that was necessary for this new life that came as an unexpected gift from God. We also gave him the middle name, Jonathan, which means "gift of God," because certainly that is what he is.

Love You Forever

For our light and momentary troubles are achieving for us an eternal glory that far outweighs them all. So we fix our eyes not on what is seen, but on what is unseen, since what is seen is temporary, but what is unseen is eternal.

2 Corinthians 4:17-18, NIV

The day-to-day struggles, concerns, and inconveniences that we deal with in having a new baby are here today and gone tomorrow. Whatever we have sacrificed—be it steps in our career, the security of a full bank account, space in our homes, schedules, our bodies—all of it is for an eternal investment that has no end. From God's perspective, a human baby is a spiritual being who has eternal value.

Our relationship with Christ is of utmost importance as we realize the everlasting quality of life. In this life and in the next, God invites us to live close to Him. While on earth we have the Holy Spirit to surround us, and in heaven we will be face-to-face with God. Trying to understand this blows my mind, but as I think of raising a child from a baby into young adulthood, it is clear that in loving a baby we are helping another person start their life well-grounded in love. Out of that love grows security, trust, and, eventually, the ability for that person to return love.

The well-known psychologist Erik Erikson breaks down our lives into phases of developmental tasks. The task of a baby is to learn to trust. Erikson says that an infant comes into the world asking the question, "Can I trust? Or must I mistrust?" A baby who learns to trust, because of consistent love, comfort, and having their needs met, has a much better chance of feeling secure. When they are satisfied with the answer to this question, they are prepared to delve into the next developmental level, which your darling two-year-old will remind you is to attain autonomy. But before the wonderful "twos" arrive filling your ears with the words "I can do it myself," know that you are investing in work with everlasting consequences. To love a baby is to begin the process of equipping them for life. As each level of growth builds on the previous one, providing security for a newborn is the foundation on which all developmental levels stand.

As moms, God has entrusted us with this unique and responsible role, but He hasn't left us to do it by ourselves. Just as we nurture our little one through the various stages of human growth, God is with us providing what we need to get the job done. He does this through friends, caring family members, and the power of His Holy Spirit. What we must do is keep our eyes fixed, not on what is seen (our own tendency toward incompetence,) but on what is unseen, our loving and faithful God. (2 Corinthians 4:18). May God bless all your efforts, imperfect but faithful mother.

Blessing the Babies… and Their Parents

The LORD bless you and keep you;
the LORD make His face to shine on you
and be gracious to you; the LORD turn His face
toward you and give you peace.

NUMBERS 6:24-26, NIV

These ancient words of blessing, first spoken by Aaron in the Old Testament, are often repeated for infants in a church or synagogue. In our congregation, it is a high and holy moment when moms and dads bring their little ones forward for the pastor to bless and to speak aloud the parents' wishes to raise their children in faith. Whether it's a baby dedication, baptism, or blessing, every person in the congregation leans in, craning necks to catch a glimpse of the sweet child held by parents who hope their baby doesn't squawk too loudly. The baby is welcomed into the congregation as the church family stands up to promise their help in teaching this child about God's unfailing love.

When my husband and I were the parents holding our little ones before the waters of baptism, I reflected on our children's place in our family, sandwiched between ancestors who reach back to generations of Scandinavian farmers and forward to descendants yet unnamed. For me the baptism of our babies reminded me of the cloud of witnesses in our family tree, who cheer us on in faith and who created a legacy of prayer and trust in God. I also felt the support of the congregation behind us, pledging to love and bless our children.

We all need blessing. Not just the baby in our arms, but as parents who feel the tremendous responsibility for raising children well, we find ourselves in great need. But what does blessing really mean? Recently, while hanging out with extended family, a niece who is now old enough to become a mother herself registered her dislike of the word, "blessing." Perhaps it's the over-use of the word that gets under her skin, as it does mine, but the word itself is full of goodness, meaning God's favor and protection. This is what I desire for my children.

When an infant is dedicated or baptized or blessed, everyone from old to young gives full attention to the child, not wanting to miss the sweet cooing noise or cry the baby might make. We are naturally drawn to the newly born. There is something so special about their freshness and innocence, their complete dependency on others to survive. We admire their smooth skin, their round chubby cheeks, the unspoiled stare from clear eyes that know no guilt.

While we sense our lives have progressed far from the days our own innocence, I hope we are able to realize we are loved by God. We may or may not have been held up before a congregation to have Aaron's blessing spoken on our behalf, but God's blessing is for each of us today. As we look at the beautiful face of a baby, who is a child of God, may we remember that we are all children of God as well, and He looks at us with such love. As infants are dependent on parents to thrive, we parents are dependent on God for His favor and protection. On our own we are flawed creatures that tend to get lost in our selfish ways.

We desperately need blessing! So, to you—mother of a newborn—take heart and receive the old but relevant words of blessing that are spoken for you:

The LORD bless you and keep you;
(May God grant you His favor and protection)

May the LORD make His face
shine on you and be gracious to you;

May the LORD turn His face
toward you and give you peace.

Amen.

Bonnie Sparrman is grateful for how being a mother has enriched her life. She and her husband, Eric, have three children of their own and one who joined the family as a German exchange student. Johanna, Bjorn, Karl-Jon, and Isabel, are past the baby-stage, but lessons they taught their parents are worth remembering.

Bonnie is also a registered nurse, writer, culinary instructor, corporate team builder, and consummate baker, who believes that fresh cardamom bread goes a long way to promote friendship and love.

Bonnie is frequently found in the kitchen, welcoming guests—reading, hiking, swimming or cycling the trails that circle the lakes of Minneapolis with her biking buddy, Eric. For Bonnie, a stellar morning is biking to a friend's house with a batch of warm muffins in her backpack.